BRIGHTON & HOVE ALBION

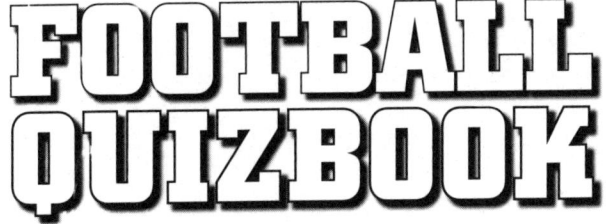

FOOTBALL
QUIZBOOK

BRIGHTON & HOVE ALBION
FOOTBALL QUIZBOOK

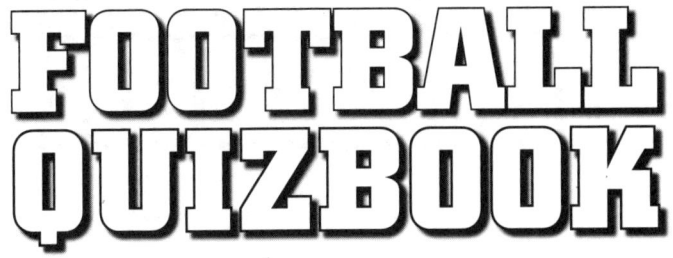

PAUL BRINKHURST

BRIGHTON & HOVE ALBION

FOOTBALL QUIZBOOK

All statistics, facts and figures are correct as of 1st August 2008

© Paul Brinkhurst

Paul Brinkhurst has asserted his rights in accordance with the Copyright, Designs and Patents Act 1988 to be identified as the author of this work.

Published By:
Pitch Publishing Ltd,
A2 Yeoman Gate,
Durrington BN13 3QZ

Email: info@pitchpublishing.co.uk
Web: www.pitchpublishing.co.uk

First published 2008

A catalogue record for this book is available from the British Library.

10-digit ISBN: 1-9054113-4-0
13-digit ISBN: 978-1-9054113-4-4

Printed and bound in Great Britain by Cromwell Press

INTRODUCTION

Brighton & Hove Albion Football Quizbook covers every aspect of the100-years-plus history of the club. It will also act as an excellent reference book of the club's facts and figures.

The book includes questions on all aspects of Brighton & Hove Albion's history, including club records, legends, stadiums, transfers, cup competitions, opponents, scores and key games.

Fans will be tested to find out how much they really know about the history of the club. With 100 themed quizzes there's something to challenge all fans and if you want to show off your knowledge of the club then this book is the one for you.

It's a book that I hope will be used for quizzes at home and in the pub and to generate discussions and debates.

I hope you enjoy reading this quiz book as much as I enjoyed writing it and that it brings back some wonderful memories about the club.

ACKNOWLEDGEMENTS

I would like to thank all those at Pitch Publishing who have helped in getting this book published.

Special thanks to Brighton historian Tim Carder, who co-wrote *Seagulls* and the *Albion A-Z* with Roger Harris, which proved useful books to refer to when writing the quizzes. Tim also proved invaluable in verifying and checking all the quizzes and for this I am extremely grateful.

Thank you also to all the other authors of Brighton & Hove Albion related books which I referred to at certain times when writing the book. Also thank you to Paul Camillin, the Albion press officer, for his help and advice and in organising the pictures for the book.

Finally, thanks to my wife Angela and daughter Alice for their patience and support.

Quiz 1 – HISTORY OF THE CLUB

1. Which player holds the record for making the most league appearances, 509 between 1922 and 1936?

2. What ground did the club play at before the Goldstone?

3. What year was the club formed?

4. Our record capped England player won three caps during 1982, which player?

5. In what year 1910, 1915 or 1920 was our first football league game (v Southend)?

6. In what season were we runners up in the FA Cup?

7. In 1978-1979 we achieved our best ever season in the Football League Cup, which round did we reach?

8. In 2003-2004 we gained our only promotion via the play offs, who did we beat in the final?

9. In what year was our last ever league game played at the Goldstone?

10. Who was the club's first manager, Frank Scott-Walford, John Jackson or John Robson

Quiz 2 – CLUB RECORDS

1. Who was the club's record home attendance of 36,747 against in 1958?

2. Peter Ward is the club's record league goalscorer in a season, 1976-77, how many goals did he score?

3. Who did we pay a then record transfer fee of £500,000 to Manchester United for in 1980?

4. In 1965 we recorded our record FA Cup victory in the competition proper, 10-1 against which team?

5. Who is our youngest ever league player?

6. Who in 1958 was our record league defeat, 9-0, against – Manchester United, Middlesbrough or Newcastle United?

7. Who holds the record for the most league goals in total aggregate?

8. Which Welsh club did we record our joint record league victory against in 1951?

9. In July 2003 we received a record transfer fee of £1,500,000 for Bobby Zamora from which club?

10. True or False. In 1955-56 a club record was set when the team scored 112 league goals?

Quiz 3 – MANAGERS

Match the manager with their period in charge.

1. Brian Clough	1951-1961
2. Micky Adams	1947-1951
3. Jimmy Melia	1973-1974
4. Chris Cattlin	2002-2003
5. Barry Lloyd	1982-1983
6. Alan Mullery	1987-1993
7. Billy Lane	1983-1986
8. Pat Saward	1970-1973
9. Steve Coppell	1999-2001
10. Don Welsh	1976-1981

Quiz 4 – NUMBERS

All the answers are numbers.

1. What are the most goals scored in a football league match by a Brighton player?

2. How many players have played in the World Cup finals while signed on for Brighton?

3. The highest ever position was in 1981-82 in Football League Division 1, in what position did the club finish?

4. What was Bobby Zamora's squad number in his last season at Brighton?

5. How many goals did Brighton concede against Notts County in the 1991 play-off final?

6. How many goals were scored in the second half of a league game v Walsall in 1976?

7. The quickest ever league goal was scored by Maheta Molango in how many seconds – 8, 10 or 12?

8. The most penalties conceded by Brighton in a game was against Crystal Palace, how many?

9. How many goals did Brighton concede in their first ever home league match in the First Division v Arsenal in 1979?

10. How many times has Alan Mullery managed the club?

Quiz 5 – NATIONALITIES

Match the player with their country of birth.

1. Paul Reid	France
2. Dirk Lehmann	Malta
3. Stefan Iovan	South Africa
4. Moshe Gariani	West Germany
5. Hans Kraay	Romania
6. Ivar Ingimarsson	Australia
7. Denis Foreman	Argentina
8. Seb Carole	Israel
9. Glen Geard	Holland
10. Federico Turienzo	Iceland

Quiz 6 – ON THIS DAY

Identify the event in the club's history by the date.

1. 24th June 1901

2. 28th August 1920

3. 18th April 1951

4. 25th December 1957

5. 21st May 1983

6. 26th April 1997

7. 7th August 1999

8. 13th April 2002

9. 30th May 2004

10. 24th July 2007

Quiz 7 – POT LUCK

1. What was the phrase uttered by radio commentator Peter Jones on 21st May 1983 that is known as a famous saying in the club's history?

2. In 1997 who did the club play in the Fans United Day?

3. Who won the Player of the Season award in both 1979-1980 and 1992-1993?

4. Who was the first English professional to score in the new millennium?

5. Which Scottish born manager managed the club between 1963-1968?

6. Who played for the club in the 1970s and managed it in the 1990s?

7. Which player was known as the Football Genius in the late 1980s and early 1990s?

8. Who did the club sell to Celtic for £1,500,000 in 2005?

9. What is the largest attendance to watch a Brighton game?

10. Who is the only player to play three times for Brighton at Wembley Stadium?

Quiz 8 – WHERE DID WE GET HIM?

Where did we sign the following players from?

1. John Byrne

2. Richard Carpenter

3. Bert Murray

4. Peter O'Sullivan

5. Dean Saunders

6. Jimmy Langley

7. Alan Duffy

8. Teddy Maybank

9. Paul Reid

10. Guy Butters

Quiz 9 – GUESS WHO?

1. I was born in Scotland in 1954 and made my debut for Brighton in 1980 before leaving in 1984 to join Manchester City.

2. I finished as top goalscorer for the club in 1987-88 with 32 goals.

3. I made my debut for Brighton in 1996-1997 and was still at the club in 2008-2009.

4. I was born in 1941; I played for England and was appointed Brighton manager in 1976.

5. I signed for Brighton in 1987 and my previous clubs include West Ham United, Birmingham City, Aston Villa and Charlton Athletic.

6. I was born in 1953, I first joined the club in 1987, my son played for the club in 1998-1999 and I was still involved in 2008-2009.

7. I was born in 1930, made my debut in 1952 and made 247 consecutive appearances for the club.

8. I made my debut for Brighton in 1977; I am a goalkeeper and made 98 appearances for the club.

9. I finished as top league goalscorer for the club in 1992-93 with 20 goals.

10. I played at Wembley on more than one occasion for the club and my son was in the first team squad at the start of the 2008-2009 season.

Quiz 10 – BOOK THAT MAN

All questions on Albion-related books.

1. Who were the authors of *Seagulls* and the *Albion A-Z*?

2. What was the name of the book on the troubles of 1995-1997 written by Stephen North and Paul Hodson where football fans united to save Brighton?

3. John Vinicombe wrote three Brighton-related books – *Up, Up and Away*, *Super Seagulls* and what?

4. Paul Camillin and Stewart Weir wrote *Albion – the first 100 years* to celebrate the clubs centenary. What was the name of Paul's second Albion-related book?

5. Who wrote the book *A Few Good Men*?

6. Complete the name of the book by Stewart Weir and Paul Hayward – *More than* ....?

7. Bennett Dean, Paul Hazlewood, and Simon Levenson wrote about two seasons, two Championships, what was the book called?

8. Who wrote the Brighton book *A Portrait in Old Picture Postcards*?

9. What was the name of the book Mike Ward wrote on "How he learned to love Brighton & Hove Albion"?

10. Dan Tester wrote which Albion-related book?

Quiz 11 – BOBBY ZAMORA

1. In what year was Bobby born in Barking – 1980, 1981 or 1982?

2. Who did Bobby make his debut against when he joined Brighton on loan from Bristol Rovers?

3. Which Brighton manager handed Bobby his debut at Withdean?

4. How much did Bobby initially cost when he signed in August 2000 – £50,000, £100,000 or £150,000.

5. In 2000 Bobby scored his first hat trick for Brighton in a 7-1 away win against which club?

6. In total how many league goals did Bobby score for Brighton in his 125 league appearances – 66, 76 or 86?

7. How many times did Bobby win the club's player of the season award?

8. Which club did Bobby sign for in July 2008 after having previously played at Tottenham and West Ham United since leaving Brighton in 2003?

9. Brighton fans used to have a chant they would sing for Bobby, to which singer's song called *That's Amore*?

10. After leaving Brighton Bobby turned down the opportunity to play for which country in the 2006 World Cup?

Quiz 12 – PETER WARD (WARDY)

1. In what year was Wardy born? – 1955, 1956 or 1957?

2. Who did Brighton sign Wardy from?

3. Who did Wardy make his debut against where he scored in the first minute?

4. Which Brighton manager gave Wardy his debut?

5. What club record did Wardy set in the 1976-1977 season?

6. In 1977 Wardy was selected for England Under 21s at the Goldstone and scored a hat-trick against which country?

7. How many times did Wardy win the club's official player of the season award?

8. Against which club did Wardy make his only full international appearance against?

9. When Wardy left Brighton in 1980 which club did he join?

10. In his second spell at the club in 1982-1983 Wardy scored his last goal for the club against whom – Manchester United, Watford or Newcastle United?

Quiz 13 – CHARLIE WEBB

1. Before joining Brighton Charlie had enjoyed success by helping which Sussex based non-league team to a treble?

2. In what year did Charlie make his debut against West Ham United? – 1909, 1915, or 1919?

3. Charlie scored the winning goal in the Charity Shield against which team?

4. How many appearances did Charlie make for Brighton – 265, 275 or 285?

5. What was unique about his appointment as manager?

6. During his 28 years as manager he was offered the job at which top London club?

7. Which country did Charlie represent at international level?

8. True or False – Charlie had two benefit games whilst at the club?

9. Who replaced Charlie as Brighton team manager in 1947?

10. Which two teams played in the 1949 benefit game for Charlie?

Quiz 14 – MICKY ADAMS

1. In which county was Micky born in 1961 – Lancashire, Sussex or Yorkshire?

2. Which London club did Micky first take charge as a manager?

3. When Micky joined Brighton in 1999 who joined him as Assistant Manager?

4. In what season did Micky lead Brighton to the Division Three title?

5. Which club did Micky leave Brighton to join as Assistant Manager in October 2001?

6. Which of these clubs did Micky not play for during his career – Gillingham, Leeds United, West Ham United or Southampton?

7. Which team did Micky guide to promotion in 2002-2003?

8. What club was Micky's last as a manager prior to returning to Brighton in 2008?

9. Who was Micky's first signing on returning to Brighton for the 2008-2009 season?

10. Who was Micky's first game back at Withdean against in July 2008?

Quiz 15 – ROBBIE REINELT

1. Who did Brighton sign Robbie from?

2. How much did the club sign Robbie for – £15,000, £25,000 or £35,000?

3. Which Brighton manager signed Robbie?

4. Who did Robbie make his Brighton debut against?

5. True or False – Robbie never scored more than one goal in a league game for Brighton?

6. What did Robbie do on 3rd May 1997 that he will be remembered for in the club's history?

7. What was the name of the sponsor on the club shirts on that day in May 1997?

8. Who did Robbie replace when he came on as substitute in the crucial game on 3rd May 1997?

9. Robbie scored his last league goal for Brighton in April 1998 against a team nicknamed the "Stags", which team?

10. When Robbie left Brighton in 1998 which club did he join?

Quiz 16 – TOMMY COOK

1. Who did Tommy make his Football League debut against in 1922?

2. Tommy scored a record 123 league and cup goals for the club which included how many hat-tricks, also a club record?

3. Which county did Tommy represent at cricket?

4. Tommy won his only England cap in 1925; he was the club's only England cap until May 1980 when who also represented England?

5. Who did Tommy make his England debut against?

6. Tommy's benefit game in 1927 was played against which team?

7. How many appearances did Tommy make for the club – 109, 209 or 309?

8. Which other Football league team did Tommy play for after leaving Brighton?

9. True or False – Tommy never managed Brighton?

10. What was the title of the Albion fanzine produced in 1995 where the title paid tribute to him?

Quiz 17 – GARY STEVENS

1. As a schoolboy which league club did Gary join?

2. In what season did Gary make his Brighton debut?

3. Who was the goalkeeper in the game Gary made his debut?

4. How many league goals did Gary score for Brighton in his career – 2 , 12 or 22?

5. Who was manager when Gary made his Brighton debut?

6. Gary made 152 appearances for Brighton, in which year did he win the player of the season award?

7. What was the last game Gary played for Brighton?

8. Which club did Gary sign for when he left Brighton?

9. How many full England caps did Gary win – 7, 17 or 27?

10. When Gary retired from playing through injury in 1992 which club was he playing for?

Quiz 18 – STEVE FOSTER

1. Where did Brighton sign Steve from in 1979?

2. What award did Steve win in both 1979-1980 and 1992-1993?

3. Who did Steve captain when he won the League Cup in 1988?

4. How many full England caps did Steve win?

5. What was the trademark that most football fans associated with Steve?

6. Who did Steve replace in the team for the 1982-1983 Cup Final replay after missing the original game through suspension?

7. When Steve left Brighton in 1984 which club did he sign for?

8. Steve later rejoined Brighton for a second spell in 1992 after playing the previous season for which team?

9. In total how many appearances goals did Steve make for Brighton – 232, 282 or 332?

10. Who were the opponents in Steve's testimonial game in 1996?

Quiz 19 – FA CUP 1982-83

1. Which team did Brighton beat 1-0 in the third round after a replay?

2. Who scored the winning goal in the third round tie?

3. In the fourth round who did Brighton beat 4-0 with Michael Robinson scoring twice?

4. What was the score when Liverpool were beaten at Anfield in round 5?

5. Who scored the goals in the win against Liverpool?

6. Who did Brighton beat 1-0 at home in round 6?

7. Who was officially appointed manager on 16 March 1983 after leading Brighton to the semi finals?

8. At which stadium was the semi final played?

9. Who played in goal in the semi final win against Sheffield Wednesday?

10. Who were the club sponsors during the cup season?

Quiz 20 – LEAGUE CUP

1. In 1969 Brighton lost 3-2 at home to which first division club in round 3?

2. In 1976-1977 Brighton beat two first division teams on their way to the fourth round, name one of them?

3. A crowd of 33,500 watched Brighton draw at home before losing the replay to which team in the fourth round in 1976-1977?

4. The club's best performance in the league cup was in 1978-1979 when they reached which round?

5. Which team did they lose to that year?

6. Since the early 1980s the cup has been named after its sponsor, what was the name of the cup in the 1981-1982 season?

7. Which league two team did Brighton lose to in 2005-2006?

8. Who did Brighton lose 1-0 to in the 2007-2008 competition?

9. Who did Brighton play in the first round of the 2008-2009 competition?

10. What is the name of the sponsors for the 2008-2009 season?

Quiz 21 – FA CUP

1. Which player in the 1982-1983 Cup Final team later became manager of Brighton in 1995?

2. In 1979-1980 Brighton lost to the same team in the League Cup and FA Cup, which team?

3. 35,000 watched Brighton draw at home before losing the replay to which team in the fourth round in 1966-1967?

4. The club reached the fifth round in 1983-1984 before losing to which team?

5. In 1929-1930 Brighton reached the fifth round before losing 3-0 in front of 56,469 people away to which North East club?

6. In 1995-1996 Brighton lost to which league team 4-1 on penalties after drawing 0-0 after extra time?

7. Which non-league team did Brighton lose to in 1996-1997?

8. True or False – Brighton beat Shoreham 12-0 and Brighton Amateurs 14-2 in the 1902-1903 competition?

9. Who did Brighton play in the first round of the 2007-2008 competition?

10. What is the name of the FA Cup's sponsor for the 2008-09 season?

Quiz 22 – OTHER CUPS

1. Who were the sponsors in 2007-2008 of the Football League Trophy in which Brighton lost to Swansea City 1-0?

2. Who beat Brighton in the 2006-2007 Football League Trophy competition?

3. In 2007-2008 Brighton won the Sussex Senior Cup by beating which team 1-0 in the final?

4. Name one of the two teams Brighton played in the 1979-1980 Tennant Caledonian Cup?

5. In the FA Youth Cup 2007-2008 which Premier League club's team beat Brighton?

6. In 1980-1981 Brighton beat Maccabi Nethanya 2-0 at home to win which cup?

7. Who did Brighton reserves lose to in the 2006-2007 Pontins Holiday Combination Championship play-off final?

8. Which ex-Brighton player reached the semi final of the UEFA Euro 2008 Championships?

9. Which future Brighton player captained Steaua Bucharest in the 1986 European Cup Final?

10. Which ex Brighton player scored the winning goal in the 2007-2008 FA Trophy Final for Ebbsfleet United?

Quiz 23 – FA CUP SCORES

Match the FA Cup game with the score.

1. v Torquay United 2007-2008   Won 8-0

2. v Rushden & Diamonds 2001-2002   Lost 2-1

3. v West Ham United 2006-2007   Won 1-0

4. v Norwich City 1982-1983   Won 6-2

5. v Northwich Victoria 2007-2008   Lost 1-0

6. v Walton & Hersham (rep) 1973-74 Won 2-0

7. v Mansfield Town 2007-2008   Won 3-0

8. v Aldershot 2000-2001   Lost 3-0

9. v Coventry City 2005-2006   Won 2-1

10. v Stafford Rangers 2006-2007   Lost 4-0

Quiz 24 – THE 1900s to 1920s

1. What was the name of the founder of Brighton and Hove Albion in 1901?

2. In 1902-1903 Brighton gained promotion to Division One of the Southern League after a play-off win against which team now known as the Hornets?

3. In 1910 the team won three trophies – the Southern Professional Charity Cup, the Southern League Championship Shield and which other trophy?

4. Who joined the club in 1909 at the start of a career that was to span two world wars and five decades as a player and manager?

5. Which minor first team league did Brighton win in the 1913-1914 season?

6. Who made his debut in 1906 and went on to make 443 appearances for the club?

7. In 1921-1922 which player scored Brighton's first twelve goals of the season?

8. In 1920-1921 the club played in what newly formed division?

9. In 1925-1926 how much to the nearest pound was a season ticket to the ground – £1, £3 or £5?

10. The 1920s saw the first Brighton player to win an England cap and who also scored eight hat-tricks for the club. Which player?

Quiz 25 – THE 1930s

1. In 1929-1930 which two strikers formed a lethal partnership, scoring 63 goals in league and cup games?

2. Why did the club play in the qualifying rounds of the 1932-1933 FA Cup?

3. Which London club beat Brighton in the fifth round of the FA Cup in 1932-1933?

4. Who managed the club throughout the 1930s?

5. True or False: The club purchased the freehold of the Goldstone Ground during the 1930s?

6. Who scored 23 league goals in 1934-1935, and also in 1933-1934 finished top scorer with 15 goals despite playing only the last 10 games?

7. Identify these opponents in 1935-1936 by their nicknames then – The Cobblers, The Biscuitmen?

8. In the mid 1930s the club were linked with a move to which stadium in Hove?

9. In 1938-1939 Brighton finished third in Division 3 South. Which Welsh team finished as Champions?

10. Which west country team were Brighton's last opponents in September 1939 before war was declared?

Quiz 26 – THE 1940s

1. Brighton lost 18-0 to which team on Christmas Day 1940 in a wartime game?

2. True or False. Brighton's wartime game v Southampton in September 1940 was abandoned after three minutes?

3. In what league did Brighton play in during the 1941-1942 season?

4. What was unique about the FA Cup ties in 1945-1946?

5. In 1944-1945 a team later to be known as the Royals beat Brighton 9-3 and 3-2, which team?

6. Who scored 21 wartime league goals in 1945-1946?

7. In 1947-48 where did Brighton finish in Division 3 South?

8. As a boy, Chairman Dick Knight won a national competition for sports writing which referred to which Brighton player?

9. Who finished top league goalscorer in the 1948-1949 season?

10. Who managed the club from November 1947 into the 1950s?

Quiz 27 – THE 1950s

1. In April 1951 the club recorded their record league victory against which team? The record was later equalled in 1965-1966.

2. Which player joined the club from Leeds in 1953 and left for Fulham in 1957 and went on to play for England?

3. Who finished top league goalscorer in the 1953-1954 season?

4. In 1954 Brighton attracted their first home league gate of over 30,000 against which South Coast rivals?

5. Who was club chairman between 1951-1958?

6. Who scored 28 league goals in 1955-1956?

7. In 1955-1956 Brighton finished second to which team in Division 3 South after scoring a club record 112 goals?

8. Who am I? During the 1953-1954 season to the 1956-1957 season I played every league game and eventually made 247 consecutive league and cup appearances.

9. Which team finished second when Brighton won Division 3 South in 1957-1958?

10. In 1958-1959 Brighton lost 9-0 away to Middlesbrough. Which future Brighton manager scored 5 goals in the game?

Quiz 28 – THE 1960s

1. Who was goalkeeper for much of the 1960s and went on to play over 380 games for the club?

2. In 1961 Brighton played the reigning league champions in the FA Cup, which team?

3. Which manager was in charge at the start of the 1964-1965 season?

4. In 1964-1965, when the club finished as Fourth Division Champions, who did they beat in the final league game?

5. Which player joined the club in May 1964, only six months after playing for England?

6. Which comedian was a director of the club during the 1960s?

7. Who finished top league goalscorer in 1965-1966?

8. In November 1965 the team scored 10 goals in one game and then two weeks later scored 9, against which teams?

9. What were the Christian names of the two players in the late 1960s who shared the same surname and went on to make over 500 appearances between them?

10. In 1969-1970 32,539 watched Brighton lose at home in the league cup to which team?

Quiz 29 – THE 1970s

1. Who became manager in June 1970?

2. In 1971 which player was signed with the aid of the Buy-A-Player Fund?

3. Who did Brighton finish runners up to in the 1971-1972 season?

4. Who finished as top goalscorer with 12 league goals in 1973-1974?

5. In what position did Brighton finish in the league during 1975-1976 – 3rd, 4th or 5th?

6. Which two teams gained promotion with Brighton from Division 3 in 1976-1977?

7. Which ex-Leicester City player played all 46 league games for Brighton during the 1976-1977 season?

8. In 1978 which two Peruvian internationals did the club give trials to?

9. In 1977-1978 Brighton narrowly missed promotion, who finished as Division 2 champions?

10. Who finished top league goalscorer when Brighton gained promotion to Division 1 in 1978-1979?

Quiz 30 – THE 1980s

1. Who finished top league goalscorer in the 1980-1981 season with 19 goals?

2. Which player was sold to Queens Park Rangers in 1981 for £300,000?

3. Which player made the most league appearances in the 1982-1983 FA Cup final season?

4. In 1983-1984 a centre half and forward had the same surname, what name?

5. In 1984 which ex-England striker signed for the club having played at Southampton the previous season?

6. In 1985-1986 Brighton lost to which local rivals in the FA Cup sixth round?

7. Who finished top league goalscorer in the 1986-1987 season when the club were relegated?

8. Who am I? I signed on a free transfer in the 1980s, was sold for £60,000 and later in my career clubs paid a combined total of over £10 million pounds for me.

9. In 1987-1988 when Brighton gained promotion back to Division 2, three players played all 46 league games. Name one of them?

10. Which future award-winning author played for Brighton in the late 1980s and was top league goalscorer in 1987-1988?

Quiz 31 – THE 1990s

1. Who did Brighton beat in the 1990-1991 play off semi-final?

2. In 1991-92 Brighton were relegated from Division 2 with two other teams. Name one of them?

3. Who finished as top league goalscorer in 1992-1993 and 1993-1994?

4. Which goalkeeper did Brighton sell to Leeds United in April 1993?

5. Which goalkeeper made 44 league appearances in 1995-1996?

6. Against which team was the home game abandoned in April 1996?

7. In 1996-1997 Brighton did their only league double against the "Monkey Hangers", who were they?

8. In 1996-1997 who wore the number 2 shirt in the final game at the Goldstone?

9. Which was the first season Brighton played home games at Gillingham?

10. Who arrived as manager in April 1999?

Quiz 32 – THE 2000s

1. Which goalkeeper signed from Bristol Rovers in June 2000?

2. Which manager left the club and later joined Hull City as manager?

3. Who finished top league goalscorer in the 2003-2004 season with 25 goals?

4. Which player was referred to as the Coca Cola kid after a supporter won a competition to buy a player?

5. In November 2006 which player scored a hat trick against Northwich Victoria in an 8-0 FA Cup win?

6. Which Premiership club knocked Brighton out of the FA Cup in January 2007?

7. In the "Back to Back" championship teams, which midfield player's squad number was 12?

8. What position did Brighton finish in League One in 2007-2008?

9. In 2007-2008 which player left the club to sign for Brentford?

10. Which two players were released at the end of the 2007-2008 season but were to later gain one year contracts for 2008-2009?

Quiz 33 – NAME THE YEAR

1. FA Cup Runners Up

2. Division Two Play-Off Winners

3. Division Four Champions

4. First game at Withdean

5. Bobby Zamora signs for Tottenham Hotspur

6. Gary Hart testimonial game against Charlton Athletic

7. Peter Ward made debut

8. Division Three (South) Champions

9. Last game at Goldstone

10. Charity Shield Winners

Quiz 34 – PICTURE 1

Identify these Legends?

1.

2.

3.

4.

5.

6.

7.

8.

9.

10.

Quiz 35 – PICTURE 2

Who am I?

1.

2.

3.

4.

5.

6.

7.

8.

9.

10.

Quiz 36 – WITHDEAN

1. In what season did the club play their first league game at Withdean?

2. Who did the club play in a friendly in the first game at Withdean?

3. Who scored a hat-trick in the first league game at Withdean against Mansfield Town?

4. Who were the first away team to win at Withdean?

5. What was the first season the club gained promotion while playing at Withdean?

6. Who was the first Brighton player to score two penalties in a game at Withdean?

7. Brighton also scored six goals at Withdean in September 2000 against which team?

8. In 2003-2004 what was the last game Brighton played that season at Withdean?

9. In 2004 the stadium was renamed for one game to launch a new album by Fatboy Slim. What was the stadium called?

10. In 2007 8,691 set a new attendance record and watched Brighton play which team at Withdean?

Quiz 37 – GOLDSTONE GROUND

1. Which other club did Brighton share the Goldstone with in the early 1900s?

2. In what year did the ground host a football match between Afghanistan and Luxembourg in the Olympic Games?

3. In what year was the largest attendance at the Goldstone?

4. In which year was the first game played under floodlights at the Goldstone, 1955, 1961 or 1965?

5. Who were the opponents when England played the only under 21 international to be played at the Goldstone in 1977?

6. Who was the last Brighton player to score a hat-trick at the Goldstone?

7. What was the area at one stage fenced off in the centre of the East Terrace known as?

8. In 1996 who were the opponents when a game was abandoned after a pitch invasion?

9. Who were the last two league games played against at the Goldstone?

10. In what month of the year was the last game played at the Goldstone?

Quiz 38 – FALMER

1. Which District Council contested the decision to approve planning permission for Falmer?

2. Part of which University campus is required for part of the stadium site?

3. What was the name of the referendum campaign in 1999 launched by various Brighton supporters groups?

4. Which manager resigned at the end of the 2001-2002 season citing the lack of a permanent stadium as one of the main reasons behind his decision?

5. Who was the Deputy Prime Minister who initially approved the plans in 2005 before a legal challenge was mounted?

6. What was the name of the political party set up by supporters in 2006?

7. What is the name of the road that the Stadium will be linked to?

8. Who was the Secretary of State for Communities and Local Government who confirmed a yes decision to the planning applications in July 2007?

9. In March 2008 Chief Executive Martin Perry said the stadium was due to open in time for which season?

10. Approximately what is the planned capacity of the stadium – 22,000, 24,000 or 26,000?

Quiz 39 – KEEPERS

1. Which keeper made a record 386 appearances for Brighton?

2. Which of these legends was a keeper – Johnny McNichol, Eric Gill or Des Tennant?

3. How many consecutive clean sheets did keeper Bill Hayes keep in 1923-1924?

4. Who was sold to Leeds United in 1993 for an initial payment of £350,000?

5. Michel Kuipers first played for which English club?

6. Guess Who? I made 160 appearances in goal and left to join Oldham Athletic in 1990.

7. Who was the starting keeper in the first game at Withdean?

8. Which keeper featured in the book *A Few Good Men*?

9. Which of these managers was a keeper – Jeff Wood, Barry Lloyd or Steve Gritt?

10. Which keeper made 320 appearances and was known by the nickname 'Pom Pom'?

Quiz 40 – DEFENDERS

1. Which defender joined Brighton from Portsmouth in 1979 and played for England while at the club?

2. Who made over 480 appearances between 1962 and 1974 and is referred to as "Sir" by some Brighton fans?

3. Who wore the number 6 shirt in the drawn FA Cup final game against Manchester United?

4. Which attacking fullback was nicknamed "Rubber Legs" in the 1950s?

5. Which of these international players was a defender – Tommy Cook, Jack Jenkins, or Jack Doran?

6. Which left back featured in the book *A Few Good Men*?

7. Guess Who? I made over 180 appearances and made my Brighton debut in 2002.

8. Which defender made his debut as a 16-year-old and was voted Player of the Season in 1995-1996?

9. Who became Micky Adams' first signing in his second spell as manager in May 2008?

10. Who did Brighton sell for £900,000 in 1981?

Quiz 41 – MIDFIELDERS

1. Dave Turner joined the club from which team in 1963?

2. Which player joined in 2000 and made over 250 appearances and was known by the nickname "Chippy"?

3. Which midfielder played aged 41 in 1995?

4. Who in 2002 became the only captain to lead Brighton to two Championships?

5. Which midfielder signed from Luton Town made 11 international appearances for the Republic of Ireland while with the club?

6. Which midfielder's squad number for the 2007-2008 season was number 22?

7. Guess Who? I made over 300 appearances mainly in midfield and made my debut in 1988 after signing from Barnet.

8. Which midfielder joined the club permanently in 1984 from Nottingham Forest after a successful loan spell at the club?

9. Who was sold to Colchester United in 2008 for £250,000?

10. Which popular player was named after Queens Park Rangers' 1973 squad?

Quiz 42 – GOALSCORERS

**Match the player with the number of league
and cup goals he scored for Brighton.**

1. Kit Napier	25
2. Bert Stephens	95
3. Kurt Nogan	123
4. Fred Binney	28
5. Tommy Cook	39
6. Peter Ward	79
7. John Byrne	44
8. Gerry Ryan	96
9. Garry Nelson	99
10. Tony Towner	60

Quiz 43 – CRYSTAL PALACE

1. In the famous Palace vs. Brighton match in 1989 that featured five penalties awarded by referee Kelvin Morton, who was the successful scorer of the Seagulls' penalty?

2. Which defender who was born in Singapore in 1960 played for both Brighton and Palace during the 1980s and 1990s?

3. Who was the controversial referee who took charge of the FA Cup 1st round 2nd replay between the two clubs in the 1976-1977 season?

4. In 2007-2008, which ex-Palace midfielder joined Brighton from Falkirk?

5. Who was credited in the press as scoring the winning goal for Brighton in their 1-0 win at Selhurst Park on 18th October 2005?

6. And, who scored Palace's last minute winner in their 3-2 win at Withdean in the same 2005-2006 season?

7. Which Palace player was responsible for breaking the leg of Gerry Ryan in a match between the two sides in the 1980s?

8. Which former Brighton player scored for Palace in both an FA Cup semi-final and an FA Cup final?

9. Can you name three managers who have managed both Brighton and Palace since 1980?

10. Which goalkeeper was loaned from Palace to Brighton during the 2006-2007 season?

Quiz 44 – NICKNAMES

Identify the opponents by the nickname.

1. The Canaries

2. The Cobblers

3. The Royals

4. The Hatters

5. Cottagers

6. Valiants

7. The Os

8. The Owls

9. Black Cats

10. The Saddlers

Quiz 45 – GROUNDS

Who would we be playing at these grounds?

1. Glanford Park

2. Sixfields Stadium

3. Edgar Street

4. Sincil Bank

5. Keepmoat Stadium

6. Underhill Stadium

7. Liberty Stadium

8. Prenton Park

9. Edgeley Park

10. Bramall Lane

Quiz 46 – TRANSFERS – IN

Which club did the following players join Brighton from?

1. Gary Hart

2. Glenn Murray

3. Mark Lawrenson

4. Charlie Oatway

5. Andy Whing

6. Stuart Storer

7. Gordon Smith

8. Steven Thomson

9. Colin Kazim-Richards

10. Nicky Forster

Quiz 47 – TRANSFERS – OUT

**Match the player with the club they joined
after leaving Brighton.**

1. Danny Cullip	Swansea City
2. Dean Saunders	Yeovil Town
3. Leon Knight	Southampton
4. Darren Currie	Oxford United
5. John Byrne	Leeds United
6. Frank Worthington	Ipswich Town
7. Kurt Nogan	Sheffield United
8. Nathan Jones	Tranmere Rovers
9. Jimmy Case	Burnley
10. Seb Carole	Sunderland

Quiz 48 – HOW MUCH?

Match the player with the fee paid by Brighton.

1. Mark Lawrenson	£75,000
2. John Gregory	Free
3. Teddy Maybank	£400,000
4. Glen Murray	£111,111
5. Ian Mellor	£238,000
6. Andy Ritchie	£300,000
7. Peter Ward	£40,000
8. Guy Butters	£4,000
9. Nicky Forster	£250,000
10. Gordon Smith	£500,000

Quiz 49 – NATIONALITIES 2

Match the player with their country of birth.

1. John Robinson	Singapore
2. Michel Kuipers	United States
3. Jacob Cohen	Australia
4. Rami Shabaan	Zimbabwe
5. David Adekola	France
6. Eric Young	Nigeria
7. Alistair Edwards	India
8. Alexandre Frutos	Israel
9. Eric Lancelotte	Holland
10. Junior McDougald	Sweden

Quiz 50 – SQUAD NUMBERS

**Match the squad number to the player
in the 2007-2008 season.**

1. 14   Gary Hart

2. 5   Guy Butters

3. 17   Nicky Forster

4. 22   Shane McFaul

5. 12   Glenn Murray

6. 19   Tommy Fraser

7. 9   Joel Lynch

8. 4   Adam El-Abd

9. 31   Jake Robinson

10. 6   Adam Hinshelwood

Quiz 51 – LEAGUE POSITIONS

Match the season with Brighton's final league position.

1. 2006-2007	4th
2. 2005-2006	1st
3. 2004-2005	23rd
4. 2003-2004	17th
5. 2002-2003	14th
6. 2001-2002	16th
7. 1999-2000	24th
8. 1998-1999	11th
9. 1994-1995	20th
10. 1993-1994	18th

Quiz 52 – WHAT WAS THE SCORE?

1. Manchester United
– Division 1 November 1982 – home

2. Mansfield Town
– Division 3 August 1999 – home

3. Crystal Palace
– Championship October 2005 – away

4. Sheffield Wednesday
– FA Cup April 1983 – neutral

5. Bristol Rovers
– Division 3 December 1973 – home

6. West Ham United
– FA Cup January 2007 – away

7. Leeds United
– League 1 March 2008 – away

8. Tottenham Hotspur
– FA Cup January 2005 – away

9. Liverpool
– FA Cup February 1983 – away

10. Arsenal
– Division 1 August 1979 – home

Quiz 53 – PLAYER OF THE SEASON

Match the player with the season
he won the award.

1. 2003-2004   Kurt Nogan

2. 2002-2003   John Keeley

3. 1998-1999   Guy Butters

4. 1994-1995   Eddie Spearritt

5. 1993-1994   Steve Foster

6. 1988-1989   Graham Moseley

7. 1984-1985   Danny Cullip

8. 1979-1980   Norman Gall

9. 1973-1974   Gary Hart

10. 1972-1973   Peter Smith

Quiz 54 – 2007-2008 RESULTS

Match the game with the score.

1. v Leeds United (h)	Won 4-2
2. v Walsall (a)	Drew 1-1
3. v Leyton Orient (a)	Lost 2-0
4. v Gillingham (h)	Won 1-0
5. v Oldham Athletic (a)	Drew 2-2
6. v AFC Bournemouth (h)	Won 3-0
7. v Bristol Rovers (h)	Lost 1-0
8. v Port Vale (a)	Drew 0-0
9. v Nottingham Forest (h)	Won 2-1
10. v Crewe Alexandra (h)	Won 3-2

Quiz 55 – MORE THAN 4

**What was the score when we scored
more than four goals?**

1. Walsall home 1976-1977?

2. Wisbech home 1965-1966?

3. Halifax Town away 1971-1972?

4. Bristol Rovers away 1959-1960?

5. Notts County home 1964-1965?

6. Hartlepool United home 1996-1997?

7. Newport County home 1950-1951?

8. Charlton Athletic home 1983-1984?

9. Chester City away 1999-2000?

10. Aldershot Town away 2000-2001?

**Choose from 5-0, 5-0, 5-4, 6-0, 6-2, 7-0,
7-0, 7-1, 9-1, 10-1**

Quiz 56 – MANAGERS 2

Match the manager with their period in charge.

1. Steve Gritt	2003-2006
2. Jeff Wood	1981-1982
3. Jimmy Case	1901-1905
4. Liam Brady	1999
5. Mike Bailey	1998-1999
6. Martin Hinshelwood*	1905-1908
7. Brian Horton	1993-1995
8. John Jackson	1995-1996
9. Frank Scott-Walford	1996-1998
10. Mark McGhee	2002

* exclude periods as caretaker manager

Quiz 57 – UNSUNG HEROES

1. Who in 2000 was appointed the Poet in Residence for the club?

2. Who in the cast section of the book *Build a Bonfire* was described as an undertaker and co-founder of the *Gull's Eye* fanzine?

3. Which two unsung heroes expressed their thanks from the rostrum as the supporters' club won the FSF Services to Supporters Award in 2004?

4. Who in 1997 became Chairman of the Club?

5. What was the name of the new initiative the club introduced in July 2008 for young supporters aged up to 16 years old which was split into Gully's Gang and Team Stripes?

6. Who was named "Fan of the Year" at the 2008 Football League Awards?

7. Who edits the *Albion Almanac* and is recognised as the Club Historian?

8. Who was club secretary whilst the club were in exile at Gillingham?

9. Which fund was born from the terrorist attacks in New York on September 11th 2001 and supports youngsters from 5-16 who may not otherwise be given the opportunity or resources to play football?

10. What is the name of the registered charitable arm of the football club that works in the community?

Quiz 58 – GARY HART

1. Where was Gary born – Hornchurch, Harlow or Harwich?

2. Who was the manager that first signed Gary for Brighton in 1998?

3. Up until the 2007-2008 season what number shirt did you associate Gary with?

4. In what season did Gary score his first league goal against Torquay United?

5. Who was Gary's manager at the start of the 2001-2002 season?

6. The biggest attendance Gary played in front of was 65,167, against who?

7. Against who was Gary was sent off for the sixth time while playing for the first team in the 2007-2008 season?

8. How many league goals did Gary score for Brighton in the 2005-2006 season?

9. In Gary's top team of players he played alongside whom did he select as the manager in his testimonial brochure?

10. Which team did Brighton play against in Gary's testimonial in July 2008?

Quiz 59 – APPEARANCES

Match the player with the number of appearances for Brighton.

1. Dean Wilkins	488
2. John Keeley	331
3. Peter Ward	252
4. Ian Chapman	491
5. John Byrne	199
6. Norman Gall	375
7. Peter O'Sullivan	150
8. Steve Burtenshaw	160
9. Gerry Ryan	110
10. Ian Mellor	227

Quiz 60 – HAT-TRICKS

**Match the hat-trick hero with the
opponents he scored against.**

1. Alex Revell	Mansfield Town
2. Craig Maskell	Bradford City
3. Ian Mellor	Newcastle United
4. Darren Freeman	AFC Bournemouth
5. Jimmy Case	Colchester United
6. Danny Wilson	Torquay United
7. Gordon Smith	Walsall
8. Bobby Zamora	Coventry City
9. Bryan Wade	Charlton Athletic
10. Paul Emblen	Hartlepool United

Quiz 61 – KERRY MAYO

1. In which year did Kerry make his league debut for the club – 1995, 1996 or 1997?

2. Which Brighton manager handed Kerry his debut?

3. In 1998 Kerry scored two goals in an away game at Meadow Lane, which team was this against?

4. What was the nickname Kerry was given linked to the colour of his hair?

5. Which team is Kerry remembered for scoring an own goal against in a crucial game in 1997?

6. In what year was Kerry born – 1975, 1977 or 1979?

7. What squad number did Kerry wear during the 2007-2008 season?

8. True or False – Kerry has never won the Player of the Season award?

9. Who was Kerry's testimonial game against in 2007?

10. Which manager released Kerry from the club in May 2008 although this proved short-lived as Kerry was offered another contract by new manager Micky Adams in July 2008?

Quiz 62 – JIMMY CASE

1. From which team did Brighton sign Jimmy when he first signed?

2. In what year did Jimmy sign for Brighton – 1980, 1981 or 1982?

3. Who was the manager who first signed Jimmy for Brighton?

4. Which London team did Jimmy make his Brighton debut against?

5. In the FA Cup run in 1982-1983 which was the only round on route to the final that Jimmy failed to score in?

6. Jimmy scored a hat-trick in a 7-0 win against which team in 1983?

7. In what year was Jimmy born – 1952, 1954 or 1956?

8. Who did Jimmy sign for in March 1985 when he left the club?

9. Which manager persuaded Jimmy to rejoin the club in December 1993?

10. Jimmy was sacked as manager in December 1996 after defeat by which team known as The Quakers?

Quiz 63 – NEWCASTLE
5th MAY 1979

1. What was the score in this crucial game that clinched promotion to the first division?

2. Who scored for Brighton?

3. Two players played in the game that later went on to manage Brighton, Brian Horton was one but who was the other?

4. Who played in goal for Brighton?

5. Who were the two Welsh internationals that played for Brighton in the game?

6. Who was the Brighton substitute?

7. Who played left back in the game for Brighton to complete all 42 league appearances for the season?

8. What colour shirts did we wear in the game?

9. Who was Manager?

10. Who won Division 2 that season?

Quiz 64 – FA CUP FINAL 1982-1983

1. Which Brighton manager led us to the final?

2. Who did we play in the final and what was the score in the replay?

3. Who scored for Brighton in the first game?

4. Which Brighton player missed the first game due to suspension but played in the replay?

5. Which Brighton player went off injured in the first game?

6. Name the Brighton substitute for both games?

7. The brother of which Brighton manager scored in the final for Manchester United?

8. Brighton flew to the final courtesy of which sponsor?

9. True or False – No goals were scored in extra time in the first game?

10. Can you name six of the starting team for the replay?

Quiz 65 – PLAY OFF FINAL 1990-1991

1. Who did Brighton play in the final?

2. Who scored for Brighton?

3. Who was the manager of the opponents?

4. Which Romanian played for Brighton in the final?

5. Who played in goal for Brighton in the final?

6. Name the Brighton captain in the final?

7. Name the two Brighton substitutes?

8. What were the main two colours of Brighton's kit?

9. What was the attendance – 59,940, 69,940 or 100,000?

10. What was the score?

Quiz 66 – DONCASTER
26th APRIL 1997

1. What was the score in this crucial game that ultimately helped the club avoid relegation?

2. Who scored the last ever goal at the Goldstone for Brighton?

3. Which Brighton player was sent off in the game?

4. Who played in goal for Brighton?

5. What was the attendance in the game – 9,341, 11,341 or 15,341?

6. Name the only Brighton substitute used that day?

7. What music was played by a trumpeter just before kick off?

8. True or False – The winning goal was scored at the South Stand end of the ground?

9. Who was Manager?

10. Who were the kit suppliers for Brighton – Admiral, Ribero or Adidas?

Quiz 67 – HEREFORD UNITED
3rd MAY 1997

1. What was the name of the ground where the game was played at?

2. What was the final score?

3. Which Brighton player deflected a cross into his own goal?

4. What was the score at half time?

5. Who was the manager of the opponents?

6. Gary Hobson came on as substitute for who?

7. Who wore the number 10 shirt for Brighton and finished as the club's top league goalscorer in 1996-1997?

8. Who scored the Brighton equaliser?

9. Who made a crucial save in the last minute to deny Hereford a winner?

10. What colour shirts did we wear in the game?

Quiz 68 – PLAY OFF FINAL 2003-2004

1. Which team did Brighton beat to reach the play-off final?

2. In which stadium was the final played?

3. Who was the manager of opponents Bristol City?

4. Who scored the winning goal for Brighton?

5. Who played in goal for Brighton in the final?

6. Name the Brighton captain in the final?

7. Name the two substitutes Brighton used in the game?

8. Can you name the referee for the final?

9. What was the attendance – 55,167, 65,167 or 75,167?

10. Name the three unused Brighton substitutes?

Quiz 69 – ALAN MULLERY

1. Which two London clubs did Alan play for in his career?

2. In which year did Alan first join Brighton as manager?

3. To what position did Alan guide Brighton in his first season in charge?

4. Can you name the striker Alan signed from Hartlepool during the 1977-1978 season?

5. How many full international caps did Alan win for England – 25, 35 or 45?

6. In the promotion season of 1978-1979 which Republic of Ireland international did Alan sign from Derby County?

7. In Alan's first season in charge in Division 1 in 1979-1980 which European Champions did Brighton complete the double over?

8. Who did Alan join as manager after leaving Brighton in 1981?

9. In 1986 Alan rejoined the club after the dismissal of which manager?

10. Following his departure in January 1987 Alan held various jobs before becoming Director of Football at which club during 1996-1997?

Quiz 70 – MARK LAWRENSON

1. Where did Brighton sign Mark from?

2. How much did Brighton sign Mark for – £55,555, £111,111 or £222,222?

3. In what season did Mark make his Brighton debut?

4. Who was Chairman of Brighton when Mark signed?

5. Guess the team? Mark made his Brighton league debut against these South Coast rivals and scored his first goal against the same team in the return fixture.

6. Which country did Mark make 39 international appearances for?

7. In what season did Mark get voted Player of the Season while at Brighton?

8. When Mark left Brighton in 1981 which club did he join for £900,000?

9. True or False? – Mark won one European Cup winner's medal?

10. At which club did Mark start his brief managerial career?

Quiz 71 – IAN CHAPMAN

1. In what year was Ian born – 1968, 1970 or 1972?

2. Who did Ian make his Brighton debut against at the age of 16?

3. Was Ian predominantly left or right footed?

4. Ian was the first graduate of the FA's National School of Excellence to play in the Football League. In which village in Shopshire was the school based?

5. In which season did Ian win the Player of the Season award?

6. Ian scored 4 league goals in 1994-1995, name one of the teams he scored against?

7. In Ian's last season, 1995-1996, what was the name of the sponsor on the club shirts?

8. Which manager released Ian in 1996?

9. Which team did Ian join for the 1996-1997 season?

10. Which Sussex County League team did Ian manage before returning to coach Brighton in 2006?

Quiz 72 – GARRY NELSON

1. Which team did Brighton sign Garry from?

2. Who was the manager who signed Garry for Brighton?

3. In his first season at Brighton who was his strike force partner that had been signed from Reading?

4. In which season did Garry finish top league goalscorer for Brighton with 22 league goals?

5. In 1988-1989 Garry was the one of two players to play all 46 league games, name the other player?

6. True or False – Garry scored more than 50 league goals for Brighton?

7. Which club did Garry sign for on leaving Brighton in 1991?

8. Name two teammates in the 1990-1991 Brighton squad that were also to sign for the club that Garry joined in 1991?

9. Name two league clubs beginning with the letter 'S' that Garry played for during his career?

10. After finishing his playing career Garry wrote two football books chronicling playing seasons. One book was called *Left Foot Forward*, name the other book?

Quiz 73 – BRIAN HORTON

1. Where did Brighton sign Brian from?

2. Which Brighton manager signed Brian?

3. How much did Brian cost when he signed in 1976 – £17,000, £27,000 or £37,000.

4. What was Brian's nickname?

5. Who did Brian make his debut against in 1976?

6. In what season was Brian voted Player of the Season?

7. How many appearances did Brian make for Brighton – 232, 242 or 252?

8. When Brian left Brighton in 1981 which club did he join?

9. Who did Brian succeed as Brighton manager in 1998?

10. When Brian left the club in 1999 which club did he join to manage?

Quiz 74 – PETER O'SULLIVAN

1. What nationality is Peter?

2. Can you name the club that Brighton signed Peter from?

3. Who was the manager that signed Peter for Brighton?

4. How many full international caps did Peter win for his country?

5. What award voted for by the supporters did Peter win in 1977-1978?

6. True or False – Peter scored over 50 league goals for Brighton?

7. During April 1980 Peter signed for which team before later in the year re-signing for Brighton?

8. How many appearances did Peter make for Brighton – 391, 451 or 491?

9. Who did Brighton play in Peter's testimonial game in 1980?

10. Which club did Peter sign for when leaving Brighton in 1981?

Quiz 75 – NORMAN GALL

1. In what year was Norman born – 1932, 1942 or 1952?

2. Which non league team did Brighton sign Norman from?

3. Which Brighton manager signed Norman?

4. How many times did Norman win Player of the Season?

5. In what position did Norman mainly play for Brighton – defender, midfielder or forward?

6. In 1970 Norman scored a memorable header from over 20 yards in a game at Plainmoor against which team?

7. Complete the popular chant from the terraces – "--- Norman Gall"?

8. Norman had two testimonial games while at Brighton, name one of the opponents?

9. How many appearances did Norman make for Brighton – 388, 438 or 488?

10. Which manager released Norman in 1974?

Quiz 76 – BOBBY SMITH

1. In what year was Bobby born in Yorkshire – 1930, 1933 or 1936?

2. Name the club Bobby played for before signing for Tottenham Hotspur?

3. In 1963 which European trophy did Bobby win with Tottenham Hotspur?

4. Who was the manager that signed Bobby for Brighton?

5. How many league goals did Bobby score in the 1964-1965 season with the club – 19, 21 or 23?

6. True or False – Bobby never scored a league hat-trick for Brighton?

7. What was the christian name of his namesake who played alongside him in the 1964-1965 season?

8. Why was Bobby suspended for two weeks by the club in July 1965?

9. Bobby played his last game for the club at home to the Hatters, which team was this?

10. In October 1965 Bobby left the club and joined which Sussex non-league team?

Quiz 77 – JIMMY LANGLEY

1. Which Yorkshire team did Brighton sign Jimmy from in 1953?

2. What nickname was given to Jimmy while at Brighton because of his tackling and ability to race up and down the wing?

3. In 1955 Jimmy was selected to play for England B, name the only other Brighton player to have played for England B?

4. In 1953-1954 when Brighton narrowly missed out on promotion Jimmy played in all 46 league games. Name one of two other players to also play in all 46 games that season?

5. Jimmy scored two penalties in a game against The Grecians in November 1955, who were they?

6. Which manager signed Jimmy for Brighton?

7. How many league goals did Jimmy score in his Brighton career – 4, 14 or 24?

8. In 1957 Jimmy left the club to join which team for £12,000?

9. How many full England appearances did Jimmy make?

10. With which club did Jimmy win a Third Division Championship medal and a League Cup winner's trophy in 1966-1967?

Quiz 78 – DEAN WILKINS

1. In what year was Dean born in Hillingdon – 1960, 1962 or 1964?

2. Which team did Brighton sign Dean from when he first joined the club in 1983?

3. What is the name of the elder brother of Dean who made over 80 appearances for England?

4. Which manager re-signed Dean for Brighton in 1987?

5. In 1987 Dean rejoined Brighton from PEC Zwolle after playing in which country?

6. In March 1990 Dean scored two goals at home against The Bantams, who were they?

7. Against which team in the 1990-1991 season did Dean score a last minute free-kick to clinch a play off place for Brighton?

8. Who did Brighton play in Dean's testimonial in 1995?

9. Who did Dean replace as Brighton manager in 2006?

10. In his only full season as manager in 2007-2008 before being replaced by Micky Adams what league position did Dean guide Brighton to?

Quiz 79 – ERIC GILL & GLEN WILSON

1. Eric made his debut in 1952 against the visitors from Brisbane Road, who were they?

2. Who was the manager that signed Eric?

3. How many appearances did Eric make for Brighton – 196, 296 or 396?

4. What season was Eric part of the Championship-winning team?

5. In 1958 Eric set what club record?

6. Glenn made his Brighton debut against The Cherries in 1949, who were they?

7. What was the name of Glenn's elder brother who also played for Brighton?

8. How many appearances did Glenn make for Brighton – 236, 336 or 436?

9. When Glenn left the club in 1960 who did he join?

10. In 1973 Glenn was caretaker manager before the arrival of which manager?

Quiz 80 – DES TENNANT & JOHNNY MCNICHOL

1. In which country was Des born in 1925?

2. In his first season Des finished top league goalscorer with how many goals – 10 , 15 or 20?

3. In 1954 which team played Brighton in a benefit game for Des?

4. True or False – Des scored 23 of his 47 goals for Brighton from the penalty spot?

5. At the end of the 1958-1959 season Des retired from playing after making how many appearances for the club – 224, 324 or 424?

6. From which club did Brighton sign Johnny in 1948?

7. Can you name the first season that Johnny was top league goalscorer for Brighton?

8. How many league appearances did Johnny make for Brighton during his career – 158, 258 or 358?

9. True or False – When Brighton signed Johnny they paid a club record fee of £5,000?

10. Which team did Johnny sign for when he left Brighton in 1952?

Quiz 81 – HARRY BALDWIN & ERNIE 'TUG' WILSON

1. In what year was Harry born in Birmingham – 1920, 1925 or 1930?

2. What position did Harry play?

3. In 1947-1948 what do Brighton fans most remember Harry for?

4. In 1950-1951 which other Brighton player had a joint testimonial with Harry?

5. Harry left Brighton in 1952 to join which non-league team?

6. What club record does Ernie currently hold?

7. On which wing did Ernie mainly play for Brighton?

8. Ernie had two benefit games while at the club, name one of the opponents?

9. Ernie made his debut against The Bees in 1922, who were they?

10. In fourteen seasons at the club Ernie scored 67 league goals, what was the most league goals he scored in one season?

Quiz 82 – SQUAD NUMBERS

**Match the squad number to the player
in the 2008-2009 season.**

1. 24	David Livermore
2. 2	Kevin McLeod
3. 14	Dean Cox
4. 16	Adam Virgo
5. 17	Steven Thomson
6. 18	Colin Hawkins
7. 23	Doug Loft
8. 11	Glen Murray
9. 8	Andrew Whing
10. 7	Tommy Elphick

Quiz 83 – PRE SEASON 2008-2009

Match the pre season game with the score.

1. v Athlone	Won 2-0
2. v Worthing	Drew 1-1
3. v Bognor Regis Town	Won 3-1
4. v Burgess Hill Town	Won 4-2
5. v Lewes	Lost 1-0
6. v Havant & Waterlooville	Won 3-0
7. v Stansted	Lost 3-2
8. v Charlton Athletic	Drew 0-0
9. v Ipswich Town	Won 4-0
10. v Luton Town	Won 4-2

Quiz 84 – COMINGS AND GOINGS 2008

1. Which player signed from Hull City in July 2008?

2. Which Welsh club did Kevin McLeod once play for?

3. Who did Guy Butters sign for in May 2008?

4. Who left the club in January 2008 to join Southend United?

5. Which defender rejoined Brighton for a third loan spell in July 2008?

6. Paul Reid joined which League One team on trial in July 2008?

7. Which ex-player joined Crawley Town in May 2008?

8. Which two Brighton players from the 2007-2008 season signed for Tranmere Rovers in July 2008?

9. Who did Adam Virgo rejoin the club from in June?

10. Which player signed included Shelbourne and Bohemians amongst his previous clubs?

Quiz 85 – INTERNATIONALS

**Name the Brighton players who played
in these international games.**

1. Australia v England	May 1980
2. Spain v N. Ireland	Dec 1988
3. Rep. of Ireland v Sweden	March 2006
4. England v Kuwait	June 1982
5. Finland v Wales	Sept 1986
6. England v N. Ireland	Feb 1982
7. Scotland v Wales	May 1976
8. England U21s v Portugal U21s	April 2002
9. England U21s v Ukraine U21s	Aug 2004
10. Romania U21s v Wales U21s	May 1992

Quiz 86 – SHIRT SPONSORS

Name the main shirt sponsors
for the following seasons.

1. 1981-1982?

2. 1983-1984?

3. 1987-1988?

4. 1990-1991?

5. 1992-1993?

6. 1997-1998?

7. 1998-1999?

8. 1999-2000?

9. 2004-2005?

10. 2008-2009?

Quiz 87 – CHARLIE OATWAY
& PAUL ROGERS

1. Which team was Charlie Oatway named after by his parents?

2. Who did Brighton sign Charlie from?

3. How many league goals did Charlie score in his first season at the club – 4, 6 or 8?

4. What number shirt did Charlie wear in the 2003-2004 play off final v Bristol City?

5. Which Hampshire non-league team did Charlie join after retiring from professional football?

6. Who did Brighton sign Paul Rogers from?

7. Which manager signed Paul for Brighton?

8. In his first season for the club Paul scored two goals away from home at Sincil Bank against which team?

9. True or False – Paul was club captain when the club gained back-to-back championships in 2001 and 2002?

10. In which season did Paul last score a league goal for Brighton?

Quiz 88 – BACK-TO-BACK CHAMPIONS

1. Which player only missed one league game during the back-to-back championships in 2000-2001 and 2001-2002?

2. Who finished top league goalscorer for the club in both seasons?

3. Which team completed the league double over Brighton in the 2000-2001 season?

4. Brighton clinched promotion in 2000-2001 after winning 2-0 away to which team?

5. Which player during 2000-2001 wore the number 12 shirt on both the first and last league games of the season?

6. In 2001-2002 Brighton lost one home league game against which club?

7. Which ex-Fulham player made 42 league appearances as centre back during the 2001-2002 season?

8. Who finished as second highest league goalscorer for Brighton during 2001-2002?

9. Who did Brighton beat 1-0 away on the last day of the season?

10. Who finished as runners up to Brighton in 2001-2002?

Quiz 89 – DIVISION 3 SOUTH CHAMPIONS 1957-1958

1. Who was the manager that led Brighton to the Division 3 South title?

2. Who made 43 league appearances as goalkeeper during the season?

3. Who signed for the club in October 1957 and later went on to manage Chelsea and Manchester United?

4. Which team did Brighton lose to 5-0 in September 1957?

5. Which player scored most league goals?

6. Which player scored 10 league goals in the season and also played cricket for Sussex?

7. Who am I? I played over 40 league games mainly as a left winger and later became groundsman for more than 28 years.

8. Which player who made 45 league appearances was part of the club for nearly 40 years as player, trainer, kit man and caretaker manager?

9. Brighton won the league on the last day of the season with a 6-0 home win against whom?

10. Who scored 5 goals in the 6-0 home win on the last day of the season?

Quiz 90 – DIVISION 4
CHAMPIONS 1964-1965

1. How much did Bobby Smith sign for from Tottenham Hotspur?

2. Who made the most league appearances?

3. How many of the 46 league games did Brighton win – 20, 26 or 30?

4. Which Brighton player was killed in a car crash during the season?

5. Which player scored most league goals?

6. In October 1964 Brighton recorded their biggest home league win of the season against which team?

7. Which former Welsh international player joined the club in October 1964?

8. True of False – Brighton scored over 100 league goals and did not lose a home league game during the season?

9. Who was player/assistant coach for the season and made only two league appearances?

10. Which team finished second to Brighton?

Quiz 91 – PROMOTION TO DIVISION 1
1978-1979

1. Which player played in 39 league games and missed the last three games after breaking his arm against Bristol Rovers?

2. Who was assistant manager to Alan Mullery during the 1978-1979 season?

3. Which player wearing number 8 scored two goals at home to Millwall in November 1978?

4. Which team did Brighton beat 5-0 in December 1978 in which Teddy Maybank scored a hat-trick?

5. How many of the 21 away league games did Brighton win – 7, 9 or 11?

6. Who was Chairman of the football club during the season?

7. Which Welsh international player scored 5 league goals during the season?

8. Brighton lost two home league games against which teams?

9. Who wore the number two shirt in the final game of the season when promotion was gained at Newcastle United?

10. Which team finished in third place behind Brighton?

Quiz 92 – POT LUCK – COUNTRIES?

Which countries were the following opponents from?

1. Steaua Bucharest
– August 1991 home – Friendly

2. Inter Zapresic
– August 1992 home – Friendly

3. Djurgarden
– March 1960 home – Albion Players Benefit Fund

4. Shelbourne
– August 1989 away – Tour

5. AS Roma
– November 1981 away – Trofeo Barilla

6. RWD Molenbeek
– August 1979 away – Dordrecht Tournament

7. Real Madrid
– August 1983 away – City of Palma Tournament

8. San Diego Sockers
– June 1983 away – Tour

9. Fluminense
– April 1960 home – Friendly

10. Tel Aviv Maccabi
– August 1966 home – Friendly

Quiz 93 – POT LUCK – GROUNDS

Who would we be playing at these grounds?

1. London Road

2. The Walkers Stadium

3. Banks's Stadium

4. Huish Park

5. Brunton Park

6. Boundary Park

7. The Galpharm Stadium

8. Elland Road

9. Sixfields Stadium

10. The Den

Quiz 94 – POT LUCK – NICKNAMES

Identify the opponents by the nickname.

1. The Hornets

2. The Rams

3. Glovers

4. The Potters

5. The Saints

6. The Quakers

7. The Terriers

8. The Tigers

9. The Iron

10. Pirates

Quiz 95 – PICTURE 3

Who am I?

1.

2.

3.

4.

5.

6.

7.

8.

9.

10.

Quiz 96 – PICTURE 4

Brighton internationals – name them.

1.

2.

3.

4.

5.

6.

7.

8.

9.

10.

Quiz 97 – KIDS 1

1. What is Brighton's nickname?

2. At which ground was did we play at in the 1982-1983 Cup Final?

3. What is the name of Brighton's mascot?

4. Where have the club played most of their home league games at?

5. What are the two main colours in our home kit?

6. What sponsors name was on the front of our shirts in the 2007-2008 season?

7. Where in the city is the new stadium being built?

8. Who was the manager when we reached the play off final in 2003-2004?

9. If we were playing against The Eagles who would we be playing?

10. Who was the Chairman when we returned to playing at Withdean?

Quiz 98 – KIDS 2

1. What position does Michel Kuipers play?

2. If we played against Pompey who would we be playing?

3. What was Dean Cox's squad number in 2007-2008?

4. True or False – Brighton have beaten Arsenal at home in the league two seasons running?

5. Which player made his 400th appearance for Brighton in 2007-2008?

6. Who did Brighton play in the 2003-2004 Division 2 Play Off Final?

7. At which team's ground did Brighton play home games at before playing at Withdean?

8. What position did Peter Ward play?

9. Which manager replaced Mark McGhee in 2006?

10. If you went to watch Brighton play at Elland Road who would we be playing?

Quiz 99 – KIDS 3

1. Complete the line of this song – "Good Old Sussex -
- --- ---"

2. Whose squad number was Number 9 in the 2007-2008 season?

3. True or False – David Beckham made his Manchester United debut against Brighton?

4. How many home league games did Brighton play in the 2007-2008 season?

5. If we were playing against the Gunners who would we be playing?

6. What position did Bobby Zamora play?

7. Which one of these teams was not in our division in 2007-2008 – Nottingham Forest, Bristol City or Leeds United?

8. Which club did Alex Revell join on leaving Brighton?

9. If you went to watch Brighton play at Selhurst Park who would we be playing?

10. How many times have Brighton won the FA Cup?

Quiz 100 – KIDS 4

Identify these players?

1.

2.

3.

4.

5.

6.

7.

8.

9.

10.

ANSWERS

Quiz 1 – HISTORY OF THE CLUB
1. Tug Wilson 2. County Ground 3. 1901
4. Steve Foster 5. 1920 6. 1982-1983 7. 5th Round where they lost 3-1 at First Division Nottingham Forest
8. Bristol City 9. 1997 v Doncaster Rovers 26 April
10. John Jackson.

Quiz 2 – CLUB RECORDS
1. Fulham 2. 32 3. Andy Ritchie 4. Wisbech Town
5. Simon Fox - 16 years 283 days 6. Middlesbrough
7. Tommy Cook 8. Newport County 9-1
9. Tottenham Hotspur – the club also received £1,500,000 for Adam Virgo from Celtic in 2005
10. True

Quiz 3 – MANAGERS
1. 1973-1974 2.1999-2001 3.1982-1983 4.1983-1986
5.1987-1993 6.1976-1981 7. 1951-1961 8.1970-1973
9. 2002-2003 10. 1947-1951.

Quiz 4 – NUMBERS
1. 5 Jack Doran & Adrian Thorne 2. 3 Steve Foster (England), Steve Penney & Sammy Nelson (Northern Ireland) 3. 13th 4. 25 5. 3 6. 7 7. 12 8. 5 9. 4 10. 2

Quiz 5 – NATIONALITIES
1. Australia 2. West Germany 3. Romania 4. Israel
5. Holland 6. Iceland 7. South Africa 8. France
9. Malta 10. Argentina.

Quiz 6 – ON THIS DAY
1. Club Formed at the Seven Stars, Ship Street 2. First Football League Game 3. Best ever victory at the time in football league 9-1 v Newport. Was later equalled in 1965 v Southend United 4. Last ever Christmas Day game 5. FA Cup Final 6. Last Game at Goldstone 7. First League Game at Withdean 8. Clinched back to back Championships 9. 2nd Division Play Off Final 10. Yes Decision announced re new stadium at Falmer.

Quiz 7 – POT LUCK
1. And Smith Must Score 2. Hartlepool United
3. Steve Foster 4. Darren Freeman 5. Archie Macaulay
6. Brian Horton 7. John Crumplin 8. Adam Virgo
9. 100,000 FA Cup Final 1982-1983 10. Steve Gatting

Quiz 8 – WHERE DID WE GET HIM?
1. Le Havre 2. Cardiff City 3. Birmingham City
4. Manchester United 5. Swansea City
6. Leeds United 7. Newcastle United 8. Fulham
9. Bradford City 10. Gillingham

Quiz 9 – GUESS WHO?
1. Gordon Smith 2. Garry Nelson 3. Kerry Mayo
4. Alan Mullery 5. Alan Curbishley
6. Martin Hinshelwood 7. Eric Gill 8. Eric Steele
9. Kurt Nogan 10. Steve Gatting

Quiz 10 – BOOK THAT MAN?
1. Tim Carder, Roger Harris 2. *Build a Bonfire*
3. *Albion: An Illustrated History of Brighton & Hove Albion FC* 4. *Brighton & Hove Albion Miscellany*
5. Spencer Vignes 6. 90 minutes 7. *We are Brighton*
8. David Ticehurst 9. *Gullhanger* 10. *Brighton & Hove Albion On This Day*

Quiz 11 – BOBBY ZAMORA
1. 1981 2. Plymouth Argyle 3. Micky Adams
4. £100,000. Brighton had to actually pay Bristol Rovers
an extra £420,000 as a result of a sell on clause in 2003.
5. Chester City 6. 76 7. 2 8. Fulham 9. Dean Martin
10. Trinidad & Tobago.

Quiz 12 – PETER WARD (WARDY)
1. 1955 2. Burton Albion 3. Hereford United
4. Peter Taylor 5. Record league goalscorer and record
league and cup goalscorer 6. Norway 7. None
8. Australia 9. Nottingham Forest 10. Newcastle Utd

Quiz 13 – CHARLIE WEBB
1. Worthing 2. 1909 3. Aston Villa 4. 275
5. He was a Prisoner of War when appointed
6. Tottenham Hotspur 7. Ireland 8. True
9. Tommy Cook 10. Portsmouth & Arsenal

Quiz 14 – MICKY ADAMS
1. Yorkshire (Sheffield) 2. Fulham 3. Alan Cork
4. 2000-2001 5. Leicester City 6. West Ham United
7. Leicester City 8. Coventry City 9. Colin Hawkins
10. Charlton Athletic – Gary Hart Testimonial

Quiz 15 – ROBBIE REINELT
1. Colchester United 2. £15,000 3. Steve Gritt
4. Carlisle United 5. True 6. He scored the equaliser at
Hereford that kept Albion in the Football League
7. Sandtex 8. Paul McDonald 9. Mansfield Town
10. Leyton Orient

Quiz 16 – TOMMY COOK
1. Queen's Park Rangers 2. 8 3. Sussex 4. Peter Ward
5. Wales 6. Gillingham. Tommy received the gate
receipts from this league game, not a separate
testimonial game as nowadays 7. 209 8. Bristol Rovers
9. False 10. The Tommy Cook Report.

Quiz 17 – GARY STEVENS
1. Ipswich Town 2. 1979-1980 v IpswichTown
3. Eric Steele 4. 2 5. Alan Mullery 6. 1982-1983
7. FA Cup Final replay 1982-1983 v Manchester
United 8. Tottenham Hotspur 9. 7 10. Portsmouth

Quiz 18 – STEVE FOSTER
1. Portsmouth 2. Brighton Player of the Season
3. Luton Town 4. Three 5. He wore white headband
6. Chris Ramsey 7. Aston Villa 8. Oxford United
9.332 10. Sheffield Wednesday

Quiz 19 – FA CUP 1982-1983
1. Newcastle United 2. Peter Ward 3. Manchester City
4. 2-1 5. Gerry Ryan and Jimmy Case 6. Norwich City
7. Jimmy Melia 8. Highbury 9. Graham Moseley
10. British Caledonian – Sponsors name did not appear
on shirts in the televised games, but they did take the
team in the helicopter to the final.

Quiz 20 – LEAGUE CUP
1. Wolverhampton Wanderers 2. Ipswich Town, West
Bromwich Albion 3. Derby County 4. Fifth
5. Nottingham Forest 6. Milk Cup 7. Shrewsbury
Town 8. Cardiff City 9. Barnet 10. Carling

Quiz 21 – FA CUP
1. Jimmy Case 2. Arsenal 3. Chelsea 4. Watford 3-1
5. Newcastle United 6. Fulham 7. Sudbury Town
8. True 9. Cheltenham Town 10. E.ON

Quiz 22 – OTHER CUPS
1. Johnstone's Paint 2. Bristol City 3. Crawley Town
4. Kilmarnock, West Ham United 5. Manchester
United 6. Jewish Chronicle 7. Ipswich Town 2-0
8. Colin Kazim-Richards also known as Colin Kazim or
Kazim Kazim 9. Stefan Iovan 10. Chris McPhee

Quiz 23 – FA CUP SCORES
1. Won 2-0 2. Won 2-1 3. Lost 3-0 4. Won 1-0
5. Won 8-0 6. Lost 4-0 7. Lost 2-1 8. Won 6-2
9. Lost 1-0 10. Won 3-0

Quiz 24 – THE 1900s to 1920s
1. John Jackson 2. Watford 3. Football Association
Charity Shield 4. Charlie Webb 5. Southern Alliance
6. Albert (Bert) Longstaff 7. Jack Doran
8. Football League Division Three South
9. £1 actually £1 1 shilling 10. Tommy Cook

Quiz 25 – THE 1930s
1. Hugh Vallance, Dan Kirkwood 2. Entry received
after deadline 3. West Ham United 4. Charlie Webb
5. True 6. Oliver Buster Brown 7. Northampton Town
and Reading 8. Greyhound Stadium 9. Newport
County 10. Bristol City – The regular season was then
abandoned and there were seven seasons of wartime
emergency football.

Quiz 26 – THE 1940s
1. Norwich City 2. True 3. London War League
4. Ties decided over two legs 5. Reading
6. Bernard Moore 7. 22nd Bottom – had to apply for
re-election 8. Johnny McNichol 9. Des Tennant
10. Don Welsh

Quiz 27 – THE 1950s
1. Newport County 2. Jimmy Langley 3. Bert Addinall
4. Southampton 5. Carlo Campbell 6. Albert Munday
7. Leyton Orient 8. Eric Gill 9. Brentford
10. Brian Clough

Quiz 28 – THE 1960s
1. Brian Powney 2. Burnley 3. Archie Macaulay
4. Darlington 5. Bobby Smith 6. Norman Wisdom
7. Charlie Livesey 8. Wisbech (10-1) and
Southend (9-1) 9. Kit and John Napier
10. Wolverhampton Wanderers

Quiz 29 – THE 1970s
1. Pat Saward 2. Bert Murray 3. Aston Villa 4. Ken
Beamish 5. 4th 6. Mansfield Town and Crystal Palace
7. Graham Cross 8. Juan Carlos Oblitas and Percy
Rojas 9. Bolton Wanderers 10. Brian Horton

Quiz 30 – THE 1980s
1. Michael Robinson 2. John Gregory
3. Gary Stevens 41 4. Young. Eric and Alan.
Also had Willie Young on loan 5. Frank Worthington
6. Southampton lost 2-0 7. Terry Connor 9 goals
8. Dean Saunders 9. Keith Dublin, Steve Gatting
and John Keeley 10. Garry Nelson

Quiz 31 – THE 1990s
1. Millwall 2. Plymouth Argyle, Port Vale
3. Kurt Nogan 4. Mark Beeney 5. Nicky Rust
6. York City 7. Hartlepool United 8. John Humphrey
9. 1997-1998 10. Micky Adams

Quiz 32 – THE 2000s
1. Michel Kuipers 2. Peter Taylor 3. Leon Knight
4. Colin Kazim-Richards 5. Jake Robinson
6. West Ham United 7. Richard Carpenter 8. 7th
9. Nathan Elder 10. Kerry Mayo and Gary Hart

Quiz 33 – NAME THE YEAR
1. 1983 2. 2004 3. 1965 4. 1999 5. 2003 6. 2008
7. 1976 8. 1958 9. 1997 10. 1910

Quiz 34 – PICTURE 1
1. Jimmy Langley 2. Bobby Zamora 3. Robbie Reinelt
4. Peter O'Sullivan 5. Charlie Webb 6. Brian Horton
7. Peter Ward 8. Mark Lawrenson 9. Alan Mullery
10. Tommy Cook

Quiz 35 – PICTURE 2
1. Micky Adams 2. Gary Stevens 3. Garry Nelson
4. Dennis Foreman 5. Bobby Smith 6. Dean Wilkins
7. Glen Wilson 8. Stuart Storer 9. Gordon Smith
10. Steve Foster

Quiz 36 – WITHDEAN
1. 1999-2000 2. Nottingham Forest 3. Darren Freeman
4. Gillingham 5. 2000-2001 6. Bobby Zamora v
Bradford City 2nd November 2002 7. Torquay United
8. Play Off Semi Final v Swindon 9. Palookaville
10. Leeds United

Quiz 37 – GOLDSTONE GROUND
1. Hove FC. Hove allowed Brighton to share. 2. 1948
3. 1958 4. 1961 5. Norway 6. Craig Maskell 1996-
1997 7. Chicken Run 8. York City 9. Wigan Athletic,
Doncaster Rovers 10. April (1997)

Quiz 38 – FALMER
1. Lewes District Council 2. University of Brighton
3. YES YES 4. Peter Taylor 5. John Prescott
6. The Seagulls Party 7. Village Way 8. Hazel Blears
9. 2010-2011 10. 22,000

Quiz 39 – KEEPERS
1. Brian Powney 2. Eric Gill 3. 7 4. Mark Beeney –
Fee eventually rose to £565,000 based on appearances
5. Bristol Rovers 6. John Keeley 7. Mark Ormerod
8. Graham Moseley 9. Jeff Wood 10. Bob Whiting

Quiz 40 – DEFENDERS
1. Steve Foster 2. Norman Gall 3. Steve Gatting
4. Jimmy Langley 5.Jack Jenkins 6. Gary Williams
7. Guy Butters 8. Ian Chapman 9. Colin Hawkins
10. Mark Lawrenson

Quiz 41 – MIDFIELDERS
1. Newcastle United 2. Richard Carpenter 3. Jimmy Case
4. Paul Rogers 5.Tony Grealish 6.Tommy Fraser
7. Robert Codner 8. Danny Wilson 9. Dean Hammond
10. Charlie Oatway. The reason behind this rather unusual
name is that both his parents were big Queens Park Rangers
fans, and decided to give their son the names of the entire
first-team squad. When his parents told his aunt the
proposed name, she said, "He'd look a right Charlie" and the
name stuck.

Quiz 42 – GOALSCORERS
1. 99 2. 96 3. 60 4. 44 5. 123 6. 95 7. 28 8. 39 9. 59
10. 25

Quiz 43 – CRYSTAL PALACE
1. Alan Curbishley 2. Eric Young 3. Ron Challis
4. Steven Thomson 5. Paul McShane 6. Jobi McAnuff
7. Henry Hughton 8. Gary O'Reilly 9. Alan Mullery,
Steve Coppell, Peter Taylor 10. Scott Flinders

Quiz 44 – NICKNAMES
1. Norwich City 2. Northampton Town 3. Reading
4. Luton Town or Stockport County 5. Fulham
6. Port Vale 7. Leyton Orient 8. Sheffield Wednesday
9. Sunderland 10. Walsall

Quiz 45 – GROUNDS
1. Scunthorpe United 2. Northampton Town
3. Hereford United 4. Lincoln City 5. Doncaster
Rovers 6. Barnet 7. Swansea City 8. Tranmere Rovers
9. Stockport County 10. Sheffield United

Quiz 46 – TRANSFERS – IN
1 Stansted 2. Rochdale 3.Preston North End
4. Brentford 5. Coventry City 6. Exeter City
7. Rangers 8. Falkirk 9. Bury 10. Hull City.

Quiz 47 – TRANSFERS – OUT
1. Sheffield United 2. Oxford United 3. Swansea City
4. Ipswich Town 5. Sunderland 6. Tranmere Rovers
7. Burnley 8. Yeovil Town 9. Southampton
10. Leeds United

Quiz 48 – HOW MUCH?
1. £111,111 2. £250,000 3. £238,000 4. £300,000
5. £40,000 6. £500,000 7. £4,000 8. Free 9. £75,000
10. £400,000

Quiz 49 – NATIONALITIES 2
1. Zimbabwe 2. Holland 3. Israel 4. Sweden
5. Nigeria 6. Singapore 7. Australia 8. France
9. India 10. United States

Quiz 50 – SQUAD NUMBERS
1. Guy Butters 2. Joel Lynch 3. Glenn Murray
4. Tommy Fraser 5. Gary Hart 6. Jake Robinson
7. Nicky Forster 8. Adam Hinshelwood
9. Shane McFaul 10. Adam El-Abd

Quiz 51 – LEAGUE POSITIONS
1.18th 2. 24th 3. 20th 4. 4th 5. 23rd 6. 1st 7. 11th
8. 17th 9. 16th 10. 14th

Quiz 52 – WHAT WAS THE SCORE?
1. Won 1-0 2.Won 6-0 3. Won 1-0 4. Won 2-1
5. Lost 8-2 6. Lost 3-0 7. Drew 0-0 8. Lost 2-1
9. Won 2-1 10. Lost 4-0

Quiz 53 – PLAYER OF THE SEASON
1. Guy Butters 2. Danny Cullip 3. Gary Hart
4. Peter Smith 5. Kurt Nogan 6. John Keeley
7. Graham Moseley 8. Steve Foster 9. Norman Gall
10. Eddie Spearritt

Quiz 54 – 2007-2008 RESULTS
1. Lost 1-0 2. Won 2-1 3. Drew 2-2 4. Won 4-2
5. Drew 1-1 6. Won 3-2 7. Drew 0-0 8. Won 1-0
9. Lost 2-0 10. Won 3-0

Quiz 55 – MORE THAN 4
1. 7-0 2. 10-1 3. 5-0 4. 5-4 5. 6-0 6. 5-0 7. 9-1
8. 7-0 9. 7-1 10. 6-2

Quiz 56 – MANAGERS 2
1. 1996-1998 2. 1999 3. 1995-1996 4. 1993-1995
5. 1981-1982 6. 2002- but also had spells as caretaker
manager 7. 1998-1999 8. 1901-1905 9. 1905-1908
10. 2003-2006

Quiz 57 – UNSUNG HEROES
1. John Baine (aka Attila the Stockbroker) 2. Ian Hart
3. Sarah Watts and Liz Costa 4. Dick Knight
5. Young Seagulls 6. Paul Samrah 7. Tim Carder
8. Derek Allan 9. Robert Eaton Memorial Fund
10. Albion in the Community

Quiz 58 – GARY HART
1. Harlow 2. Brian Horton 3. 9 4.1998-1999
5. Micky Adams 6. Bristol City in the 2004 Play Off
Final 7. Huddersfield 8. 1 9. Micky Adams
10. Charlton Athletic

Quiz 59 – APPEARANCES
1. 375 2.160 3. 227 4. 331 5.110 6. 488 7.491
8. 252 9. 199 10. 150

Quiz 60 – HAT TRICK?
1. AFC Bournemouth 2. Hartlepool United
3. Walsall 4. Mansfield Town 5. Charlton Athletic
6. Bradford City 7. Coventry City 8. Torquay United.
Bobby also scored three other hat-tricks.
9. Newcastle United 10. Colchester United

Quiz 61 – KERRY MAYO
1.1996 2. Jimmy Case 3. Notts County
4. Ginger Prince 5. Hereford United 6.1977 7. 3
8. True 9. Reading 10. Dean Wilkins

Quiz 62 – JIMMY CASE
1. Liverpool 2. 1981 3. Mike Bailey 4. West Ham
United 5. Third 6. Charlton Athletic 7. 1954
8. Southampton 9. Liam Brady 10. Darlington

Quiz 63 – NEWCASTLE 5TH MAY 1979
1. Won 3-1 2. Brian Horton, Peter Ward, Gerry Ryan
3. Chris Cattlin 4. Eric Steele 5. Peter Sayer, Peter
O'Sullivan 6. Malcolm Poskett 7. Gary Williams
8. Yellow 9. Alan Mullery 10. Crystal Palace

Quiz 64 – FA CUP FINAL 1982-1983
1. Jimmy Melia 2. Manchester United, Lost 4-0.
3. Gordon Smith, Gary Stevens 4. Steve Foster
5. Chris Ramsey 6. Gerry Ryan 7. Dean Wilkins
8. British Caledonian 9. True 10. Graham Moseley,
Steve Gatting, Graham Pearce, Tony Grealish, Steve
Foster, Gary Stevens, Jimmy Case, Gary Howlett,
Michael Robinson, Gordon Smith, Neil Smillie

Quiz 65 – PLAY OFF FINAL 1990-1991
1. Notts County 2. Dean Wilkins 3. Neil Warnock
4. Stefan Iovan 5. Perry Digweed 6. Dean Wilkins
7. Ian Chapman John Byrne 8. Red and White
9. 59,940 10. Lost 3-1

Quiz 66 – DONCASTER 26TH APRIL 1997
1. Brighton Won 1-0 2. Stuart Storer 3. Ian Baird
4. Mark Ormerod 5. 11,341 6. Robbie Reinelt
7. The Last Post 8. True 9. Steve Gritt 10. Admiral

Quiz 67 – HEREFORD UNITED 3RD MAY 1997
1. Edgar Street 2. 1-1 3. Kerry Mayo
4. 1-0 to Hereford 5. Graham Turner 6. Stuart Storer
7. Craig Maskell 8. Robbie Reinelt 9. Mark Ormerod
10. Blue and White Stripes.

Quiz 68 – PLAY OFF FINAL 2003-2004
1. Swindon Town 2. Millennium Stadium, Cardiff
3. Danny Wilson 4 Leon Knight 5. Ben Roberts
6. Danny Cullip 7. John Piercy, Paul Reid
8. Richard Beeby 9. 65,167 10. Adam Hinshelwood,
Michel Kuipers, Kerry Mayo

Quiz 69 – ALAN MULLERY
1. Tottenham Hotspur and Fulham 2. 1976
3. 2nd in Division Three and gained promotion
4. Malcolm Poskett 5. 35 6. Gerry Ryan
7. Nottingham Forest 8. Charlton Athletic
9. Chris Cattlin 10. Barnet

Quiz 70 – MARK LAWRENSON
1. Preston North End 2. £111,111 3. 1977-1978
4. Mike Bamber 5. Southampton 6. Republic of
Ireland 7. 1978-1979 8. Liverpool 9. True – Won with
Liverpool in 1984, finished as runner up in 1985
10. Oxford United

Quiz 71 – IAN CHAPMAN
1.1970 2. Birmingham City 3. Left 4. Lilleshall
5.1995-1996 6. Brentford, Bristol Rovers, Cambridge
United, Birmingham City 7. Sandtex 8. Jimmy Case
9. Gillingham 10. Whitehawk

Quiz 72 – GARRY NELSON
1. Plymouth Argyle 2. Barry Lloyd 3. Kevin Bremner
4.1987-1988 5. Gary Chivers 6. False scored 47 league
goals and 59 in all competitions 7. Charlton Athletic
8. Steve Gatting , John Robinson. Mike Small also
played for Charlton later on loan from West Ham.
9. Southend United, Swindon Town 10. *Left Foot In
The Grave*

Quiz 73 – BRIAN HORTON
1. Port Vale 2. Peter Taylor 3. £27,000 4. Nobby
5. Preston North End 6. 1976-1977 7. 252
8. Luton Town 9. Steve Gritt 10. Port Vale

Quiz 74 – PETER O'SULLIVAN
1.Welsh 2. Manchester United 3. Freddie Goodwin
4. Three 5. Player of the Season 6. False 7. San Diego
Sockers 8. 491 9. Southampton 10. Fulham

Quiz 75 – NORMAN GALL
1.1942 2. Gateshead 3. George Curtis 4. 2
5. Defender 6. Torquay United 7. Sir 8.Wolves,
Chelsea 9. 488 10. Brian Clough

Quiz 76 – BOBBY SMITH
1. 1933 2. Chelsea 3. European Cup Winners Cup
4. Archie Macaulay 5. 19 6. True 7. Jack Smith
8. Reported for pre season training overweight and
suspended for being unfit 9. Luton Town
10. Hastings United

Quiz 77 – JIMMY LANGLEY
1. Leeds United 2. Rubber Legs 3. Peter Ward 4. Eric
Gill, Glen Wilson 5. Exeter City 6. Billy Lane 7. 14
8. Fulham 9. 3 10. Queen's Park Rangers

Quiz 78 – DEAN WILKINS
1. 1962 2. Queens Park Rangers 3. Ray Wilkins
4. Barry Lloyd 5. Holland 6. Bradford City
7. Ipswich Town 8. Queens Park Rangers
9. Mark McGhee 10. 7th

Quiz 79 – ERIC GILL & GLEN WILSON
1. Leyton Orient 2. Billy Lane 3. 296 4. 1957-1958
5. Most Consecutive Appearances – 247
6. Bournemouth 7. Joe Wilson 8. 436
9. Exeter City 10. Brian Clough

Quiz 80 – DES TENNANT
& JOHNNY MCNICHOL
1.Wales 2. 10 3. Brentford 4. True 5. 424
6. Newcastle United 7. 1949-1950 8. 158
9. True 10. Chelsea

Quiz 81 – HARRY BALDWIN
& ERNIE 'TUG' WILSON
1.1920 2. Goalkeeper 3. Saved 5 successive penalties
and 7 out of 9. 4. Jack Ball 5. Kettering Town
6. Most appearances – 566 (509 League, 57 Other)
7. Left 8. Gillingham, Birmingham City 9. Brentford
10. 11 in 1934-1935

Quiz 82 – SQUAD NUMBERS
1. Tommy Elphick 2. Andrew Whing
3. David Livermore 4. Colin Hawkins
5. Glenn Murray 6. Doug Loft 7.Adam Virgo
8. Kevin McLeod 9. Steven Thomson 10. Dean Cox

Quiz 83 – PRE SEASON 2008-2009
1. Drew 0-0 2. Won 4-0 3. Won 4-2 4. Won 2-0
5. Drew 1-1 6. Won 4-2 7. Won 3-1 8. Lost 1-0
9. Lost 3-2 10. Won 3-0

Quiz 84 – COMINGS AND GOINGS 2008
1. David Livermore 2. Swansea City
3. Havant & Waterlooville 4. Alex Revell
5. Matt Richards 6. Hereford United 7. Sam Rents
8. Bas Savage and George O'Callaghan 9. Celtic
10. Colin Hawkins

Quiz 85 – INTERNATIONALS
1. Peter Ward – England 2. Steve Penney – Northern
Ireland 3. Wayne Henderson – Republic of Ireland
4. Steve Foster – England 5. Dean Saunders – Wales
6. Steve Foster – England and Sammy Nelson –
Northern Ireland. The only time Brighton players have
been on opposing sides. 7. Peter O'Sullivan – Wales
8. Bobby Zamora – England 9. Dan Harding –
England 10. John Robinson – Wales

Quiz 86 – SHIRT SPONSORS
1. British Caledonian 2. Phoenix Brewery 3. Nobo
4. Nobo 5. TSB Bank 6. Sandtex 7. Donatello
8. Skint 9. Skint 10. IT First

Quiz 87 – CHARLIE OATWAY
& PAUL ROGERS
1. Queens Park Rangers (see Quiz 41 Answer 10 for
full explanation) 2. Brentford 3. 4 4. 10
5. Havant & Waterlooville 6. Wigan Athletic
7. Micky Adams 8. Lincoln City 9. True
10. 2001-2002

Quiz 88 – BACK TO BACK CHAMPIONS
1. Paul Watson 2. Bobby Zamora 3. Southend United
4. Plymouth Argyle 5. Richard Carpenter 6. Brentford
7. Simon Morgan 8. Lee Steele 9. Port Vale
10. Reading

Quiz 89 – DIVISION 3 SOUTH CHAMPIONS 1957-1958
1. Billy Lane 2. Eric Gill 3. Dave Sexton
4. Southampton 5. Peter Harburn (20)
6. Denis Foreman 7. Frankie Howard
8. Glen Wilson 9. Watford 10. Adrian Thorne

Quiz 90 – DIVISION 4 CHAMPIONS 1964-1965
1. £5,000 2. Jimmy Collins (45) 3. 26 4. Barrie Rees
5. Wally Gould 6. Notts County 6-0 7. Mel Hopkins
8. True 9. Steve Burtenshaw 10. Millwall

Quiz 91 – PROMOTION TO DIVISION 1 1978-1979
1. Mark Lawrenson 2. Ken Craggs 3. Malcolm Poskett
4. Cardiff City 5. 7 6. Mike Bamber 7. Peter Sayer
8. Cambridge United and West Ham United
9. Chris Cattlin 10. Stoke City

Quiz 92 – POT LUCK – COUNTRIES?
1. Romania 2. Croatia 3. Sweden
4. Republic of Ireland 5. Italy 6. Belgium 7. Spain
8. USA 9. Brazil 10. Israel

Quiz 93 – POT LUCK – GROUNDS
1. Peterborough United 2. Leicester City 3. Walsall
4. Yeovil Town 5. Carlisle United 6. Oldham Athletic
7. Huddersfield Town 8. Leeds United
9. Northampton Town 10. Millwall

Quiz 94 – POT LUCK – NICKNAMES
1. Watford 2. Derby County 3. Yeovil Town
4. Stoke City 5. Southampton 6. Darlington
7. Huddersfield Town 8. Hull City
9. Scunthorpe United 10. Bristol Rovers

Quiz 95 – PICTURE 3
1. Tony Towner 2. Charlie Oatway 3. Kit Napier
4. Danny Wilson 5. Dave Sexton 6. Dennis Gordon
7. Steve Gatting 8. Barry Lloyd 9. John Byrne
10. Danny Cullip

Quiz 96 – PICTURE 4
1. Dean Saunders 2. Willie Irvine 3. Steve Foster
4. Gerry Ryan 5. Frank Worthington
6. Michael Robinson 7. Brian Cough
8. Sammy Nelson 9. Tony Grealish 10. Steve Penney

Quiz 97 – KIDS 1
1. Seagulls 2. Wembley Stadium 3. Gully
4. Goldstone Ground 5. Blue and White 6. SKINT
7. Falmer 8. Mark McGhee 9. Crystal Palace
10. Dick Knight

Quiz 98 – KIDS 2
1. Goalkeeper 2. Portsmouth 3. 7 4. True 1981-1982,
1982-1983 5. Kerry Mayo 6. Bristol City
7. Gillingham 8. Forward 9. Dean Wilkins
10. Leeds United.

Quiz 99 – KIDS 3
1. By the sea 2. Nicky Forster 3. True 4. 23 5. Arsenal
6. Forward 7. Bristol City 8. Southend United
9. Crystal Palace 10. None

Quiz 100 – KIDS 4
1. Joel Lynch 2. Dean Cox 3. Tommy Elphick
4. Kerry Mayo 5. Gary Hart 6. Guy Butters
7. Colin Hawkins 8. Nicky Forster 9. Kevin McLeod
10. Michel Kuipers